W9-BVJ-055

LEADING
WOMEN

Sandra Day O'Connor

SARAH DE CAPUA

Cavendish
Square

New York

To Dr. Craig Wilkinson—and the life-affirming staff of
Atlanta Oncology Associates

Published in 2014 by Cavendish Square Publishing, LLC
303 Park Avenue South, Suite 1247, New York, NY 10010

Copyright © 2014 by Cavendish Square Publishing, LLC

First Edition

Website: cavendishsq.com

This publication represents the opinions and views of the author based on his or her personal experience, knowledge, and research. The information in this book serves as a general guide only. The author and publisher have used their best efforts in preparing this book and disclaim liability rising directly or indirectly from the use and application of this book.

CPSIA Compliance Information: Batch #WS13CSQ

All websites were available and accurate when this book was sent to press.

Library of Congress Cataloging-in-Publication Data

De Capua, Sarah.
Sandra Day O'Connor / Sarah De Capua.
p. cm. — (Leading women)
Includes bibliographical references and index.
Summary: "Presents the biography of Sandra Day O'Connor against the backdrop of her political, historical, and cultural environment"—Provided by publisher.
ISBN 978-0-7614-4961-4 (hardcover) — ISBN 978-1-62712-117-0 (paperback)
978-1-60870-716-4 (ebook)
1. O'Connor, Sandra Day, 1930—Juvenile literature. 2. United States. Supreme Court—Biography—Juvenile literature. 3. Judges—United States—Biography—Juvenile literature. 4. Women judges—United States—Biography—Juvenile literature. I. Title. II. Series.
KF8745.O25D4 2011
347.73'2634—dc22
[B]
2011009225

Editor: Deborah Grahame-Smith   Art Director: Anahid Hamparian   Series Designer: Nancy Sabato
Photo research by Connie Gardner

Cover photo by Katie Travelstead
The photographs in this book are used by permission and through the courtesy of: *Getty Images*: 1, 43, Hulton Archive, 12, 16, David Hume Kennerly, 37, 48, Alfred Eisenstaedt, 38; Time and Life Images, 65, 67; *AP Images*: 4, 34, 56, 60, 62, 73, 76; *Corbis*: Susan Ragan, 8; Bettmann, 14, 27; *Alamy*: This Life Pictures, 30.

Printed in the United States of America

CONTENTS

CHAPTER ONE

"Justice O'Connor, Welcome."

O N FRIDAY, SEPTEMBER 25, 1981, AT JUST after 2:00 P.M., fifty-one-year-old Sandra Day O'Connor stood before Chief Justice Warren Burger in the U.S. Supreme Court building. Her husband, John, stood beside her, smiling and holding two Bibles, one stacked on top of the other. O'Connor placed her left hand on the Bibles and raised her right hand. Following the lead of Chief Justice Burger, O'Connor recited the oath of office:

> **I, Sandra Day O'Connor, do solemnly swear that I will support and defend the Constitution of the United States against all enemies, foreign and domestic; that I will bear true faith and allegiance to the same; that I take this obligation freely, without any mental reservation or purpose of evasion; and that I will well and faithfully discharge the duties of the office on which I am about to enter. So help me God.**

The chief justice shook O'Connor's hand and said, "Justice O'Connor, welcome."

The black-robed O'Connor then took her seat at the end of the left side of the bench, farthest away from the chief justice's seat. The seat on the left end is normally reserved for the newest

Sandra Day O'Connor takes the oath of office as the first woman justice of the U.S. Supreme Court, on September 25, 1981. Chief Justice Warren Burger (*left*) administers the oath, while O'Connor's husband, John, holds the family's Bibles.

member of the Supreme Court. In her book, *Sandra Day O'Connor: Justice in the Balance*, Ann Carey McFeatters wrote, "As O'Connor looked down from the bench at her husband and three grown sons, her mother and father, sister and brother . . . her eyes welled up."

It was a moment suspended in time.

[O'Connor] wrote later. The entire ceremony took only about fifteen minutes. But the brief ceremony held more than the usual importance of swearing in a new Supreme Court justice. By reciting the oath of office, Sandra Day O'Connor became the first woman justice on the Court.

O'Connor's swearing in was not just an important event in the history of the United States. It was a personal triumph for her. Nearly thirty years before, as a new graduate of Stanford University Law School in California, she was turned down for a job at every law firm to which she applied. Despite graduating among those at the top of her class of 102, the only job she was offered was as a legal secretary in a Los Angeles law firm. At the time William French Smith, one of the partners at the firm, told her she could work as a secretary, but not as a lawyer. Ironically it was Smith, the U.S. attorney general from 1981 to 1985, who would be most helpful to O'Connor when she was nominated for the Supreme Court.

Sandra Day O'Connor was born on March 26, 1930, in El Paso, Texas. She grew up on a 160,000-acre (64,750-hectare) cattle ranch that was located on the border between Texas and New Mexico. Until she was eight years old, she was the only child of Harry and Ada Mae Day. Her most frequent companions were her parents and the cowboys who worked on the ranch, which was called the Lazy B Ranch. The Lazy B had no electricity or running water until Sandra was

THE U.S. SUPREME COURT

The Supreme Court is the highest court in the judicial branch of the U.S. government. (The three branches of government are the executive, legislative, and judicial. The president is the head of the executive branch. The two-house Congress is the head of the legislative branch, and the Supreme Court heads the judicial branch.) The Supreme Court was created in 1789 by Article III of the U.S. Constitution, which states that the "judicial Power of the United States shall be vested in one supreme Court." The Supreme Court consists of the chief justice and several associate justices. Traditionally there have been eight associate justices, but the number has fluctuated between five and ten. The president nominates justices and the Senate votes on whether to confirm the nominees. Once sworn in, justices can keep their jobs for life, or until they resign or retire. Since 1790, when the Supreme Court was first convened, until early 2013, there have been a total of 112 justices. O'Connor was the 102nd justice on the Court.

The Supreme Court building, nicknamed "The Marble Palace," is located in Washington, D.C. The Court's session begins each year on the first Monday in October. The justices hear cases from October through the end of April. They announce decisions during May and June. The Court takes a break at the end of June or in early July, after it has addressed all the cases on its docket. While the justices are out of session, they may accept invitations from certain organizations or institutions to make speeches. Even while the Court is out of session, the justices' work continues; they do research and writing in preparation for the next term, which begins again on the first Monday in October.

seven. Water had to be hauled in buckets carried from an outdoor pump. In a 2000 interview, O'Connor said,

> We had to do everything ourselves. If something was broken, we couldn't call a repairman; we had to fix it. If we wanted something built, we had to build it. If we wanted something done, we had to do it. I was expected to do many things and do them well without complaint. That was obviously a good thing for me to learn. Other people depended on me doing a good job.

Without other children to play with, Sandra spent much of her free time with the ranch's horses and two thousand head of cattle. She also loved to read. "There were no other children for me to play with," she recalled in a 2005 biography. "And I didn't have a brother and sis-

ter for about ten years and was an only child in a rather god-forsaken place." In 1938, when Sandra was eight, her sister Ann was born. Brother Alan was born the following year. Although the ranch was remote and Sandra was sometimes lonely, her experiences with busy adults who sometimes didn't have much spare time to spend with her taught her to be independent. This independence prepared Sandra for a career in the law.

Young Sandra Day was approximately ten years old when this photograph was taken of her on her preferred mode of transportation around the Lazy B: horseback riding.

SANDRA DAY O'CONNOR

D. A. AND M. O.

How did Harry and Ada Mae Day come to be called D. A. and M. O.? These nicknames came from Sandra's sister Ann's attempts to spell "Dad" and "Mom." She began calling her dad D-A and her mother M-O. The names stuck. Eventually everyone in the family—and even nonfamily members—began to call Harry and Ada Mae by their nicknames.

RIDING THE RANCH

The Lazy B Ranch was located about 30 miles (48 kilometers) from any town. For Sandra and her parents, a trip to town was a special occasion. Once a week they drove to town to buy groceries and to pick up the mail. Years later O'Connor would say that her clearest memories were of driving around the ranch with her father, whom everyone, including Sandra and her siblings, called D. A. (Ada Mae was called M. O.). Sandra and D. A. would ride around the ranch, "hour after hour, bumping slowly along rocky terrain to check on a windmill or a water pipe or a tank, to see if there was a salt block out for the cattle . . . or if a cow with sore eyes was doing all right or needed some medication."

Like many children who grow up on ranches, Sandra learned to drive at a young age. She was seven. Before long her responsibilities included driving the ranch's dirt roads to bring lunch to her father and the cowboys, who were usually out branding calves, herding cattle, or repairing fences.

FAMILY HISTORY

Sandra's father, Harry Day, was the youngest of five children born to Henry Clay (known as H. C.) and Alice Hilton Day. H. C. was born and raised in Vermont, but left New England in the 1870s to make his fortune in the vast lands of the then sparsely settled West. In 1879, when he was thirty-five years old, he met and married eighteen-year-old Alice Hilton, the daughter of a rector in an Episcopal church.

In 1880 H. C. bought land in New Mexico Territory, which had recently been opened for settlement and ranching. After purchasing a herd of cattle in Mexico, he settled on his newly purchased land south of the Gila River, on what would later become the border between New Mexico and Arizona. In her book, *Sandra Day O'Connor: How the First Woman on the Supreme Court Became Its Most Influential Justice*, Joan Biskupic wrote, "The Mexican cattle had been branded on the left hip with a 'B' lying down flat—a 'lazy' B. So he named his ranch for the brand, and it endured as the Lazy B Ranch through the generations." H. C. built a house and a one-room school for his children. It was in that house that Harry Day was born in 1898. The family lived there until Harry was ten years old. Although the family moved to Pasadena, California, H. C. continued to own the Lazy B.

Young Harry went to school in Pasadena, where he was known as a bright, hardworking student and an excellent athlete who won several state swimming competitions. Harry graduated from Pasadena High School in 1918. He dreamed of attending college at Stanford University, but was drafted into World War I shortly after his graduation. (The war ended before he saw any action.) Harry's dream to attend college was once again put on hold in 1919, when his father, who was in failing health, sent him to the ranch to straighten out some of its financial issues. Harry, who was then twenty-one years old, found the dry, dusty Lazy B a terrible place to live. He hoped to stay there only long enough to make a little money and then find someone else to run it.

When H. C. died in 1921, Harry was the only one of H. C. and Alice's children who was available to take over the Lazy B for good. Harry did not want to do it. He had his own dreams to pursue, but he took on the responsibility out of a feeling of duty to his family. After a while, the life of a cattleman replaced Harry's desire to return to Pasadena and pursue college and a career. One day in the summer of 1927, he drove into El Paso to buy some bulls. While he was in town, he became acquainted with the pretty, young daughter of a fellow cattleman. They had met years earlier, but Harry had barely noticed her. This time he felt differently about her. Her name was Ada Mae Wilkey.

Sandra's mother, Ada Mae Wilkey, was born in Mexico in 1904. Ada Mae's father was W. W. Wilkey, one of seven sons who grew up in a Texas family of cattle ranchers. As a young man, W. W. took his entire savings—$100—and boarded a train, determined to ride it until his money ran out. When it did, he was in San Simon, Arizona. A local rancher gave him a one-room shack to live in and about $40 a year in exchange for tending cattle on 200 square miles (518 square km) of land. With little to spend his money on, W. W. saved everything he earned, including two $20 gold coins that two cowboys gave him in return for putting them up for a night. He later found out the "cowboys" were actually train robbers and the coins were probably stolen.

W. W. eventually saved enough money to go into the cattle business for himself. He raised calves that were sold to packinghouses, where they were butchered and shipped out across the country. It was a tough business to be in, but W. W. worked hard and earned a

Sandra Day O'Connor's grandfather, W. W. Wilkey, was a cattle rancher, like this one. It was tough and often lonely work, but Wilkey built a successful business.

good living. After a while he asked the only young woman he knew—sixteen-year-old Mamie Scott—to marry him. In a memoir of life on the ranch, called *Lazy B*, O'Connor described Mamie as a "vivacious, precocious, brown-eyed beauty."

W. W. and Mamie were living in Cananea, Mexico, when their first child, Ada Mae, was born. Soon after her birth, they moved back to Arizona and settled in a small town called Douglas. After two more children joined the family, the Wilkeys moved to Duncan, Arizona. W. W. bought the town's general store and the house next to it. He also bought a ranch north of town, as well as cattle with which to stock it. Mamie took care of the children and ran the store while W. W. ran the ranch.

According to Day family history, one day a young man named Harry Day came into the Wilkeys' general store with his parents and three siblings. Harry, who was six years older than Ada Mae, took little notice of her. However, Ada Mae was said to be instantly smitten with Harry.

Ada Mae's parents sold the general store and moved to El Paso, Texas, when Ada Mae was in high school. W. W. bought a second ranch east of town.

Ada Mae loved to play piano and sing. She was in the cast of several of her high school's musical productions. She was considered attractive and outgoing. When she graduated from high school, she enrolled at the University of Arizona, which was unusual for women at that time. After her graduation, she returned to El Paso and married a dentist, but the marriage ended in divorce (a rare occurrence in the early twentieth century) after a few months. While Ada Mae was working in El Paso as a schoolteacher, she met Harry Day again. This time he noticed her.

For the next three months, they wrote letters to one another. In one letter, Harry wrote, "I love you more than anything in the world. . . . It seems to me I have loved you always, dear, and you have always been mine." In a letter to Harry, Ada Mae wrote of her devotion to him: "I want to give you laughter and courage, ambition and fulfillment, and in that way, I shall find my own." Ada Mae's mother did not approve of the relationship, mainly because she did not want her daughter living the difficult life of a rancher's wife. Her disapproval led the couple to elope to New Mexico in 1927. The newlyweds returned to the Lazy B Ranch, where they lived together for the next fifty years. Three years after they were wed, their first child, Sandra, was born.

CHAPTER TWO

Growing Up in the West

O N THE RANCH, ADA MAE COOKED FOR HER husband and the cowboys. Because the ranch had no plumbing, she heated water for baths in a portable bathtub that was dragged into the kitchen. She washed clothes on a washboard, a corrugated rectangular surface used to scrub clothes. On the rare occasions when she had time to herself, she played the piano or read. Despite the rough, dusty life, Ada Mae took pride in looking her best. She never went outside without long sleeves and a hat, to protect her skin from the ruthless sun. She loved to wear dresses. Sometimes she drove to Lordsburg, about 20 miles (32 km) away, to get a manicure and to have her hair washed and styled.

Ada Mae subscribed to newspapers and magazines, including *Vogue*, *New Yorker*, and *National Geographic*. Having worked as a schoolteacher, she taught Sandra (and, later, Ann and Alan) to read. McFeatters wrote, "Sandra says that her mother was patient and loving and taught her to read at the age of four." The family spent evenings playing card games. In the summertime Ada Mae made homemade banana cupcakes and ice cream. McFeatters continued, "Sandra and her siblings shot quail and doves for dinner, rode horses, took picnic lunches to out-of-the-way places on the ranch, had their cousin Flournoy [Ada Mae's niece], 'like a loving older sister,' stay over" and listened to radio programs.

Taken on Easter 1940, this family photo shows Sandra (*right*) with her mother, Ada Mae (*left*), holding Sandra's brother Alan. Sandra's sister Ann is in the center.

LIKE FATHER, LIKE DAUGHTER

Harry never wanted the life of a rancher, but he learned to live with it. Through hard work and determination, he built the Lazy B into the biggest and one of the most successful ranches in the Southwest. He was a perfectionist at work and at home, and he expected his ranch hands and his family to obey him. He did not like his decisions to be questioned and, because he did all things to the best of his ability, he believed that everyone around him should do the same. He was also extremely disciplined in his spending habits. Throughout his adult life, he owned only one suit and one cowboy hat. He could be moody and depressed, and he was highly critical of Ada Mae, Alan, and, although not as often, Sandra.

Ranch hands like these were a common sight on the Lazy B. Harry required all of his employees not only to do their jobs well, but also to do them right. He didn't take shortcuts and didn't expect his employees—or his family—to take them, either.

However, he was also friendly, intelligent, and self-reliant. In her adult years, O'Connor recalled that her father "had to build a house. He had to doctor the cattle. He even doctored cowboys on occasion when something went wrong." He was also a good businessman. After paying off the ranch's debt when his father sent him there from Pasadena, Harry was determined not to incur more debt, knowing that a little debt tends to snowball into a lot of debt. Harry recognized that debt can keep people from achieving their potential, and he did not desire a financial burden for himself or his children.

One of O'Connor's most vivid childhood memories was of her father telling her to paint an unsightly screen door that was covered in peeling paint. However, she did not properly prepare the door for the new paint job by sanding it down first to remove all the chipped paint. She also neglected to protect the door's hinges by covering them with plastic or protective tape. The result of Sandra's effort looked bad. When Harry inspected the job she had done, he told her to do it again: "Because, Sandra, if you're going to do something, do it right." She spent the rest of the day taking off the new paint, sanding down the door, and repainting it. At dinner that night, she asked if he had seen her work. She expected him to be pleased. All he said was, "Yes." He did not thank Sandra or praise her. It was clear only that he expected her to do every job well.

Although O'Connor may have faced some challenging situations with her father's parenting style, it is clear that his perfectionism, perseverance, and insistence on doing things right—from running the ranch to playing card games according to the rules—rubbed off on her. She learned to fire and to clean a rifle. She learned to drive a tractor when she was ten. She learned to use tools and to brand cattle. She became independent, self-sufficient, and, like her father, a perfectionist. Her law clerks would later recall with admiration her dedicated work ethic, her attention to detail, and her absolute insistence that they do things exactly as she had instructed.

THE RADFORD SCHOOL FOR GIRLS

When Sandra was six years old, she was sent away from the ranch to El Paso, 200 miles (322 km) east, so she could attend school. Recognizing Sandra's intelligence, Harry and Ada Mae believed that their daughter could get a better education in El Paso. There she would live with Ada Mae's mother. However, as any child would, young Sandra did not like being so far from her parents. She felt confused and wondered why she had been sent away. Biskupic recalled, "As a child, Sandra could not shed the fear that her parents wanted her out of the house and might not welcome her back. It was a long and lonely existence. . . ."

Sandra attended the Radford School for Girls. Founded in 1910, it was known for its challenging academic environment. It was a boarding school, so many of Sandra's fellow students lived on campus, returning home only for holidays, school vacations, and occasional weekend visits. When these wealthy classmates returned home, they went to beautiful, spacious houses that Sandra could only dream of living in. Rather than board at Radford, Sandra lived in Grandma Wilkey's tiny bungalow. Years later Sandra described her grandmother as "an excessively talkative woman who forced her granddaughter to learn to keep out distractions as she read and studied."

Sandra returned home to the ranch at Christmas, Easter, and during summer vacations. But each time her school breaks ended, she felt once again torn away from M. O. and D. A. In her 2002 memoir, *Lazy B*, O'Connor wrote, "I climbed on board [the train] and sat at a window waving at MO and DA as the train slowly moved along the track and out of sight of my parents and the town." The lingering pain would be so great that O'Connor would say in a 1980 interview that "I dislike El Paso to this day, largely because I was homesick [as a child]."

A school picture taken at the beginning of a new school year is evidence of her unhappiness. In the photo Sandra is about ten years old. She is pictured, expressionless, alongside mostly smiling girls. Many of the girls have bows in their hair and look poised and confident. Sandra stands out because she is wearing neither a bow in her hair nor a look of confidence. Her tan, a result of spending the summer on the sun-soaked Lazy B, also stands out. It is a reminder of Sandra's rough-and-tumble ranch lifestyle, which was a contrast to the seemingly more sophisticated upbringing of the other girls. Years later a former dean of girls at the school recalled Sandra's unhappiness: "She loved riding horses and she got homesick for her family."

In this 1938-39 photo, Sandra is pictured (*standing, left*) with the other members of her class at the Radford School for Girls.

For some of her years at Radford, Sandra had her cousin Flournoy by her side. Flournoy was a year older than Sandra, and the two girls shared a room at Grandma Wilkey's, as well as many of the same school activities. But there were differences between the two. Sandra was quiet and reserved. Flournoy was outgoing and charming. Flournoy was featured in local fashion shows and was a flower girl in the weddings of a number of El Paso's most notable citizens. Biskupic described Flournoy's father's family as having a long history as "business and political leaders in El Paso, which gave Sandra some exposure to the town's upper crust as she was growing up."

HEARTACHE AND HOMESICKNESS

Even with the companionship of Flournoy and Grandma Wilkey, Sandra continued to be homesick away from the Lazy B. When she was eleven years old, an incident occurred that demonstrated Sandra's uncertainty about how she fit in: "One of my school friends said she knew something about me and my mother. 'Oh, what is that?' [I asked.] . . . 'Well,' [replied the school friend] my mother says your mother was married to somebody else, not Harry Day.' . . . I was shocked and frightened. Had I been adopted? Is that why M. O. and D. A. sent me off to school in El Paso?" Sandra asked Grandma Wilkey about the story, and her grandmother acknowledged that Ada Mae had had a brief first marriage, but reassured Sandra that Harry was indeed her father. When Sandra asked her mother about the story, Ada Mae confirmed the truth as well, but also told Sandra that it was an episode she rarely thought about because Harry was her one true love.

This incident offers a glimpse into the emotional workings of Sandra Day O'Connor. As a child she learned to keep most of her emotions to herself, rarely expressing her feelings. She grew into an equally stoic adult who focused on positives, not negatives. She rarely speaks about life in El Paso, preferring to speak and write about her life on the ranch, in spite of the fact that she spent more time away from it (nearly every school year from kindergarten through high school) than on it. Even as a grown woman, she retains unpleasant memories of her years at the Radford School. In 1996 Michael Pollack, a writer for the *New York Times*, asked a number of well-known public figures to recall and describe a piece of artwork from their school years that impressed them. Most respondents described artwork with positive connotations; it made them feel happy, free, thoughtful, or content. O'Connor, however, responded with an answer that revealed the disturbing memories she retained from her years in El Paso:

"
The artifact I remember best from my childhood was a death mask of [Mexican bandit and revolutionary] Pancho Villa. It showed his face after death, complete with a bullet wound in the forehead. It was on display at Miss Radford's School for Girls. . . . Just why it was there I never knew, but the horror of it is still part of my memory bank.
"

ANN AND ALAN

Sandra's younger sister Ann and brother Alan were also sent to live with Grandma Wilkey to attend private school in El Paso. (By then, Sandra had already graduated.) They, too, were homesick, but they did not cope with their loneliness as well as their older sister had. They expressed their feelings often to their parents, who gave in to their pleas to return to the ranch. Ann and Alan then attended "local" schools in Duncan, Arizona, 30 miles (48 km) from the ranch.

Eventually Ann earned a bachelor's degree in education from Arizona State University, and a master's degree, also in education, from the University of Arizona. She was elected to the Arizona state senate in 1990 and, in 2000, to the Pima County (Arizona) Board of Supervisors, a position she held until 2012. She was also the first woman appointed to the state's Industrial Commission. Alan earned a bachelor's degree in business administration from the University of Arizona and ran the Lazy B for thirty years.

BACK TO THE RANCH

When Sandra reached eighth grade, her parents finally gave in to her pleas to return to the ranch. Harry and Ada Mae enrolled her in the Lordsburg, New Mexico, public school. It was across the state line, but was located only about 20 miles (32 km) away. Every morning, before sunup, one of Sandra's parents would drive her over 8 miles (13 km) of the uneven dirt road that led from their home to a highway intersection, where she would wait for a bus. The bus ride to school took one hour. She would not return home until after sunset. McFeatters wrote, "By the end of the year, her parents decided the education was not worth the trouble of getting it." "Years later, when she appeared before senators at her Supreme Court confirmation hearing, O'Connor referred to this experience as a life lesson against busing to achieve racial integration in public schools. She concentrated not on the societal goal of integration but on the cost to an individual child," Biskupic reported. Having known firsthand about the rigors of long bus rides to arrive at a designated school, she recognized the toll that a similar situation could take on a student's ability to participate in after-school activities, complete homework, get a good night's rest, and concentrate in class.

The school in Lordsburg was not academically challenging enough for the gifted young Sandra, so the following school year, she returned to the Radford School for Girls. She then moved on to El Paso's Austin High School, from which she graduated in 1946, at age sixteen. Although it seems that Sandra had a number of emotional obstacles to overcome during her childhood, it could be said that the problems she faced strengthened her to face other, more difficult challenges. Brother Alan said in the early 2000s,

> **Since she was a little girl, she was never afraid of work and never afraid of a challenge. She had gone through life, instead of fighting those things or getting worn out, allowing those things to take her places other people wouldn't go.**

OFF TO COLLEGE

As she neared graduation from high school, Sandra chose to attend college at Stanford University, the same school to which her father had aspired. Harry and Ada Mae drove her to the campus in Palo Alto, California, in early September. Sandra's class, which numbered about 825 students, was the university's largest incoming class up to that time. In all, roughly seven thousand students attended Stanford. Sandra was one of only about two thousand female students.

At just sixteen years old, she was younger than most of the other students, and she felt those familiar worries about fitting in. She need not have worried. Stanford provided precisely the intellectual atmosphere that Sandra needed, and she was quickly accepted and admired by her fellow students—male and female alike.

Sandra lived in a dormitory with other girls from rural areas, one of whom was Diane Cooley, who had grown up on a prosperous ranch in Watsonville, California. In an interview for Biskupic's book, Cooley "remembered Sandra as a shy, insecure girl whose accent, a combination of Lazy B and the Radford School was different." Cooley also remembered how quickly Sandra fit in. The girls admired the

STANFORD UNIVERSITY

Founded in 1891 by California senator Leland Stanford and his wife, Jane, Stanford University was established on a site that used to be a horse farm in Santa Clara County, California, between San Francisco and San Jose. Its buildings were modeled by a famous American architect after mission buildings in nearby San Juan Capistrano. The university was designed to prepare students "for personal success and direct usefulness in life" and to "promote the public [good] by exercising an influence on behalf of humanity and civilization." Today more than 18,000 students are enrolled in the university, and Stanford is recognized as one of the world's leading institutions of higher learning.

Over the course of Stanford's long history, many of its graduates have gone on to distinguished careers in business, politics, science, and the arts. Along with Sandra Day O'Connor, Stanford's noteworthy alumni include: Ehud Barak, prime minister of Israel from 1999 to 2001; Vinton Cerf, known as the "Father of the Internet"; Eileen Collins, the first female commander of a space shuttle; Herbert Hoover, president of the United States from 1929 to 1933, and his wife, Lou Henry Hoover; Condoleezza Rice, U.S. Secretary of State from 2001 to 2005; Jerry Yang and David Filo, the founders of Yahoo!; and many U.S. senators and congressmen, as well as dozens of well-known actors and actresses.

tall, dark-haired, blue-eyed Sandra's ability to attract good-looking young men. She was also stylish. Taking after her mother, she was always well dressed, and Ada Mae and Grandma Wilkey made sure she had the latest clothing styles and accessories. As she excelled both in and out of the classroom, Sandra's social and academic status rose and her sense of inferiority diminished.

Sandra achieved high grades and spoke up in class. She did not act as if she thought she was smarter than everyone else; she simply outperformed most of her classmates. By senior year her grades, community involvement, and campus leadership earned her a membership in the Cap and Gown, an honor society for Stanford's junior- and senior-class women students. Sandra was also an enthusiastic and talented athlete who loved all kinds of sports and games. She graduated in 1950, at age nineteen, with a degree in economics.

LAW SCHOOL

Sandra entered law school at Stanford University in the autumn of 1950. She was one of only five women in the class. At the time law was a male-dominated profession, so women law students were rare. A fellow student, William Rehnquist, who had served in World War II (1939–1945) and entered law school at age twenty-five, was impressed by Sandra's confidence and ability to ask any question in class, even if it might make her sound foolish or uninformed. They attended classes in what was at the time the new law school building, which had been dedicated by Chief Justice of the Supreme Court Robert Jackson the previous summer. Interestingly Jackson was introduced to Rehnquist during that event. When Rehnquist graduated in 1952, Jackson hired him to be a law clerk. Thus Rehnquist was put on a path that led to his becoming an associate justice of the Supreme Court (in 1972). He was elevated to chief justice in 1986, a position he held until his death from thyroid cancer in 2005.

William and Sandra became friends outside the classroom. They worked on the *Stanford Law Review*, a scholarly journal focusing on legal issues that was published by the Stanford law school students. They dated briefly, seeing a few movies together. Years later O'Connor described Rehnquist as "always amusing, intelligent, with lots of interests outside of the law." The two remained lifelong friends, and Rehnquist was among those who urged President Ronald Reagan to consider O'Connor as a Supreme Court justice.

Taken about 1950, this photograph shows Sandra Day (*first row, second from left*) with her law school classmates. William Rehnquist is standing in the top row, far left.

MRS. O'CONNOR

Sandra knew she had found the man she wanted to spend the rest of her life with when she began dating John O'Connor III, a fellow law school student and the son of a San Francisco physician. In terms of family background, John and Sandra couldn't have been more different. Sandra was a country girl, from the coarse and challenging world of cattle ranching. John, born in 1930 (the same year as Sandra), was a city boy who grew up in wealth and privilege. His family was well known in San Francisco (his father had helped found Saint Francis Hospital in that city), and the O'Connors frequented the local country club.

John's law school classmates considered him handsome, with his dark hair and friendly smile. Biskupic wrote, "He enjoyed telling tales and playing jokes. But he also had drive, and, while in law school, wrote daily notes to himself about the importance of staying focused. He studied hard and after his first year became a member of the law review."

Sandra and John became better acquainted through their work on the *Law Review*. One evening, while proofreading an article together at the library, John asked Sandra to accompany him to a local diner. It was their first date. Biskupic reported that, "Afterward, neither of them dated anyone else. John later recounted to family that they went out on a date forty-one nights in a row."

Meanwhile Sandra finished law school in the spring of 1952. She completed her degree in only two years (instead of the usual three), a remarkable achievement that was a reflection of her intellectual prowess. She was twenty-two years old.

Sandra's engagement to John was announced in the *El Paso Times* on October 8, 1952. The two were married at Sandra's beloved

Lazy B Ranch on December 20 that year. Hundreds of friends, family, and neighbors attended the festive event. They dined on beef from Harry's own cows, which was cooked over pits in the ground. Sandra and John spent their honeymoon in Acapulco, Mexico.

CHAPTER THREE

Making a Name for Herself

THE NEWLYWEDS RETURNED TO STANFORD so John could complete his final semester of law school. After all of Sandra's academic successes in college and law school, and with a brand-new law degree in hand, it did not occur to her that the only job she would be offered was as a secretary at a Los Angeles law firm called Gibson, Dunn, and Crutcher. This was the encounter she had with William French Smith, who was at that time a partner in the firm. Back in the 1950s, women were still considered best at taking care of a home and family. Although some women were employed outside the home, most of them worked as secretaries, nurses, or schoolteachers. It was not until the 1960s, when the women's movement got into full swing, that women began to demand more career opportunities and salaries that equaled the pay men received.

Years later O'Connor would recall that job interview with Smith vividly:

> I was shocked. I think I was naïve. I had never stopped to think that it might be hard to get a job [because I am a woman]. The partner who interviewed me said, 'How do you type?' And I said, 'Well, fair, not great, I can get by.' He said, 'Well, if you type well enough, I might be able to get you a job as a legal secretary. But we have never hired a woman as a lawyer here. And we don't anticipate doing it.' At the conclusion of her recollection, she casually added, I declined that [job].

These women are working in an office, circa 1950s. At the time, most women who worked outside the home were secretaries, nurses, or schoolteachers.

O'Connor was growing increasingly concerned about her inability to find work. With John still finishing law school, she needed a full-time job to support them. She finally heard that the district attorney of San Mateo County (in California's San Francisco Bay area) had once hired a woman lawyer. She made an appointment with him and pleaded for a job, even if he didn't pay her. For a short time he didn't, saying he didn't have the money to hire another lawyer and didn't even have room for her in his office. She shared desk space with a secretary. McFeatters suggested, "Her determination may have sprung not just from her desperation for a job, but a hidden desire to follow her father's dream of striking out on his own in California, a state he thought offered young people a great future." In a way she did find her future. From her first day as little more than an unpaid intern, she loved being a lawyer. She found deep personal satisfaction in public service. Although she would always love visiting the Lazy B, she would never again live on the ranch, and she would not follow in her father's footsteps by running it.

Biskupic explained that O'Connor's inability to find a job that would put her law degree to good use "was not an exceptional experience. Many female, black, and Hispanic lawyers were unwelcome in the corporate legal world. O'Connor was actually more fortunate than some other law graduates, because [once John graduated] she did not have to support her family alone."

LIFE IN EUROPE

After John graduated from law school in 1953, he joined the U.S. Army to become a lawyer with the army's Judge Advocate General (JAG) Corps; he was stationed in Frankfurt, Germany. JAG lawyers are known as judge advocates and they serve primarily as legal advisers. They also serve as prosecutors for the military during courts-martial. They act as defense attorneys or as prosecutors of the military's laws. Of course O'Connor accompanied her husband to Germany. She obtained a position as a civilian (nonmilitary) lawyer with the Quartermaster Corps, a branch of the army. The corps arranged for the sale of equipment and supplies that the U.S. government had left over from World War II.

On weekends and holidays Sandra and John traveled throughout Europe and began to enjoy downhill skiing, which would become a regular part of their family vacations. In a February 1971 article for *Phoenix Magazine*, she recalled, "After John had finished his army service, we decided to stay the winter until either the money or the snow ran out. To be [safe], we bought our tickets home. Who could believe you could enjoy skiing every day for three months? Then our money and the snow ran out together and we came home."

RETURN TO ARIZONA

When they returned to the United States, it was 1957. Sandra was expecting their first child. They settled in Phoenix, Arizona's capital, instead of in more populous California. In an interview for Biskupic's book, O'Connor explained, "John and I felt that by living in Phoenix we would have an opportunity to be more actively involved with our community than might be the case if we were to return to California."[6] Postwar Arizona held a great deal of economic promise, and Sandra liked the idea of her children growing up within driving distance of the Lazy B. Harry and Ada Mae were ecstatic over their daughter's return to the area, and looked forward with great anticipation to their first grandchild.

The O'Connors already had friends who had settled in Phoenix: William Rehnquist, who was by then married to a woman named Nan, and law school friend Fred Steiner and his wife, Jacque. Thousands of people like the Rehnquists and the Steiners began flocking to Arizona after World War II. Biskupic reported, "Between 1947 and 1957, Arizona's population and economy boomed. In Phoenix alone, the population rose from 156,000 in 1945 to 450,000 in 1959. Air-conditioning made the desert areas comfortable and allowed business and industry to maintain year-round production schedules," making the region even more attractive to newcomers.

John took a job at a prestigious law firm, one of the oldest and largest in the Southwest. Sandra was unsure what kind of work she would find. One thing was certain, however: at a time when most

By the mid-1950s, Arizona, especially the Phoenix area, was booming, with new houses and impressive office buildings being constructed every week.

women were content with lives as housewives and mothers, Sandra knew that she would likely not be one of those women. Energetic and seemingly tireless, she threw herself into everything she did, usually engaging in several activities at once.

During the summer of 1957 John and Sandra rented a small apartment. According to Biskupic, "One of the first items this competitive couple bought was a [Ping-Pong] table." That fall their shared legal background drew the attention of the *Arizona Republic*, which published a feature story about them a week before they were admitted to the Arizona state bar association. On October 5, 1957, the O'Connors were sworn in to the state bar. They welcomed their first son, Scott, three days later.

SOLVING HER OWN PROBLEM

Shortly after Scott's birth Sandra turned her energies back to seeking full-time employment. However, she found that the local law firms still weren't hiring women lawyers. Undaunted, in the spring of 1958, she set up her own law firm with a partner, Tom Tobin, a University of Michigan law school graduate she had met while studying for the bar exam. Biskupic wrote, "O'Connor and Tobin rented space in a shopping center in Phoenix, alongside a grocery store, television repair shop, liquor store, and dry cleaner. It was a growing blue-collar area . . . and they both immediately joined as many local civic clubs as possible to get their names out in the community and [to] drum up business."

Their clients included grocery-store owners who were having trouble collecting on customers' grocery bills, folks with landlord-tenant problems, and people who wanted to dispute the wills of loved ones. In a 2000 commencement speech, O'Connor focused on her early years practicing law. She stressed that her cases then were not those typically considered by the United States Supreme Court.

But I always did the best I could with what I had. I learned how the law affects the average citizen and how a lawyer can help solve day-to-day problems.

STAY-AT-HOME MOM

While O'Connor settled in to life as a young lawyer and mother, she seemed to have a knack for deftly juggling the demands of her life. Years after practicing law with her, Tom Tobin said that he could not recall O'Connor ever showing up to work with baby Scott in her arms. (O'Connor was likely aware that doing so might have been viewed by clients as unprofessional.) He also recalled that O'Connor never seemed to be preoccupied by the demands of being a wife and mother. Like her own mother before her, O'Connor made everything she did look easy—even when it was not.

However, when second son, Brian, was born in 1960, even O'Connor could not maintain the juggling act of working full-time and caring for her home and family. She gave up her law practice, and for the next five years, she stayed home to raise her children. In 1962 a third son, Jay, completed the family.

DABBLING IN POLITICS

O'Connor did not really stay home. Around the time she opened her law practice with Tobin, she started to become involved in politics.

O'Connor and her family are pictured here at their Arizona home. Husband John stands beside her. Beside John is their youngest son Jay. Seated are sons Scott (*left*) and Brian.

Her first experience with a statewide campaign was the 1958 reelection bid of Arizona senator Barry Goldwater. When he successfully won reelection to the U.S. Senate with a sizable percentage of voter support, he rose to national prominence and gained a greater in-state following for his conservative ideas of small central government, fiscal responsibility, and increased individual freedom.

O'Connor campaigned on behalf of Goldwater and, after his campaign was over, she worked for the election efforts of several local Republican candidates. While she devoted time to her family, she found ways to remain socially, politically, and professionally active. She developed questions for the Arizona Bar Exam. She served on the Governor's Committee on Marriage and Family. She was an adviser

Senator Barry Goldwater greets a supporter during his 1964 presidential campaign.

to the Salvation Army. She accepted appointments to numerous county boards and panels. She volunteered in a school for black and Hispanic children. She was also an active member of many bar groups, judges' groups, and women lawyers' groups.

The O'Connors' home quickly became a community hub. Sandra and John frequently entertained friends and colleagues and held election-night parties. Biskupic noted, "She cooked the way her mother did: frequently, for many guests, and seemingly effortlessly." Their political activities made the O'Connors known to many of the state's most influential political figures. Sandra could only speculate at the time on how important those political connections would be to her future career.

In 1964 O'Connor vigorously supported Goldwater's presidential bid. He lost to Lyndon B. Johnson in the general election. O'Connor's involvement in Goldwater's campaign, however, increased her visibility among powerful Republican politicians and strategists in the state.

ASSISTANT ATTORNEY GENERAL

In 1965 O'Connor decided to go back to work as a lawyer. She did it not only because she felt the boys (ages three, five, and eight) were old enough by then to be left with a babysitter, but also because she had become so involved in community and civic affairs that she saw a law job as a welcome excuse to turn down some of her volunteer work. She recalled enjoying her responsibilities at the San Mateo County attorney's office, where she had worked for no pay following her graduation from Stanford Law School. She thought the Arizona attorney general's office would provide a similar experience—only this time she would get paid. Ideally she wanted part-time employment so she would still have time for her other activities, but it was not possible for her to secure a part-time job with the attorney general's office. The O'Connors were far from struggling financially, however. John's law career made the family prosperous. By the time of Sandra's Senate confirmation hearings, the O'Connors were worth $1 million, making Sandra one of the wealthiest people ever to be considered for the Supreme Court. Like his wife, John was an active member of the Republican Party, having joined a variety of community organizations.

Using the contacts the O'Connors had made in the Republican Party, Sandra got a job from Republican state attorney general Bob Pickrell. As an assistant attorney general, O'Connor represented state agencies and boards. As a result she widened her circle of powerful contacts. "I did the best I could in order that they would feel that I was indispensable," she said later. "Then when I told them that I very much needed to work only part-time and asked them if they wouldn't work out an arrangement for me, they then agreed to do it because, by then, they decided that they needed me even on my own terms." O'Connor's strategy demonstrated her ability to make others see her as an essential part of a business, as well as her skill at negotiating for what she wanted.

In the midst of her work, O'Connor also managed to direct the care of the boys and the home. "'My mom was definitely the caretaker of the house,' Jay, her youngest son, told Biskupic. 'She organized everything. She had help, certainly, from a maid and a babysitter, but she ran the household and figured out all the meals and all the planning.'" In the evenings, after the family had eaten dinner, the boys did their homework or participated in their sports activities. O'Connor did work she had brought home from the office or played tennis. "Recalled Jay, 'My mom would rarely flop down òn the couch.'"

STATE SENATOR

The year 1969 presented O'Connor with another excellent opportunity to use her industriousness and political connections. Newly elected president Richard Nixon was setting up his administration. He chose Arizona state senator Isabel Burgess to be on the National Transportation Safety Board. The appointment left Burgess's seat in the state senate open. O'Connor pursued the seat. She knew her chances were good. She and Burgess were friends, and O'Connor knew the members of the county Board of Supervisors, all of whom were Republicans, who would make the appointment. Although several other people expressed interest in the seat, O'Connor was selected. She filled the remainder of Burgess's term, then ran for the seat on her own in the next two elections.

When O'Connor took her seat in the legislature, wrote Biskupic, "it was the beginning of the movement in the '60s where many women around the nation were claiming more in terms of their desire to be treated equally and to have equal opportunities at work. [O'Connor] was the beneficiary, really, of a lot of that sentiment in that people were more than willing to give [her] responsibility." Republicans controlled the state legislature, and in no time, O'Connor obtained the chairmanship of an important legislative committee, as well as seats on two other powerful committees. Although others were willing to give her responsibility, O'Connor proved that she was ready to make good use of it. It had been barely twelve years since she had returned to Arizona after her years of schooling and living in Germany. Yet she had already worked her way into an impressive political position. Biskupic contended,

> " Her life until now had been a series of trade-offs and compensations: accepting the next-best job, volunteering without pay. The [state senate] appointment put her inside the corridors of power. "

She became the first woman in the nation to hold the post of majority leader in a state legislature, a position to which she was elected twice in the early 1970s.

O'Connor was well-respected in the state legislature. She quickly gained a good reputation as a hard worker and a no-nonsense legislator. McFeatters wrote, "A fellow state senator, Alfredo Gutierrez, told interviewers much later,

> " It was impossible to win a debate with her. We'd go on the floor [of the legislature] with a few facts [and try to talk others into voting with us]. Not Sandy. She would overwhelm you with her knowledge. "

William Jacquin, a former state senator who went on to head the Arizona Chamber of Commerce, told the *New York Times* that O'Connor was "a super . . . leader. She was devoted to the law . . . and was extraordinarily thorough in drafting legislation."

O'Connor also gained a reputation for being fair-minded. During her service in the state senate, she supported the Equal Rights Amendment, a proposed amendment to the U.S. Constitution that was intended to guarantee equal rights under any federal, state, or local law, regardless of gender. She helped repeal a state law that limited women to working no more than eight hours a day. (She agreed with the claims of those who supported repealing the law that it kept women out of certain high-paying jobs because of the large number of hours required to be successful in them.) She worked to provide regular mental health reviews for people who were committed to mental institutions. She supported reforms that included ensuring that state superior court judges were selected on merit, instead of on political connections. She also supported cutting state spending so that it matched revenues, which would keep Arizona from operating in deep deficits.

LETTER TO THE PRESIDENT

On October 21, 1971, at a meeting of the Phoenix Historical and Museum Commission, Phoenix mayor John Driggs, O'Connor, and other community leaders were present to discuss the preservation of various areas of Arizona's capital city. One of Driggs's aides entered the room and handed a note to him. The mayor read the note aloud and thus O'Connor heard the news that President Nixon was nominating her longtime friend, William Rehnquist, to the U.S. Supreme Court. O'Connor was surprised because Rehnquist's name had not been mentioned among those the president was considering for the nation's highest court. Rehnquist, however, had worked his own way up. He had become active in Republican Party politics in Arizona and had written speeches for Barry Goldwater's 1964 presidential campaign. When Nixon was elected president in 1968, Rehnquist had moved to Washington, D.C., to work with Arizonan Richard Kleindienst, the deputy U.S. attorney general.

William Rehnquist began his appointment as a Supreme Court justice in 1972.

Although she was happy for her old friend, O'Connor had one regret: three weeks earlier, she had written a letter to President Nixon suggesting that he name a woman to one of the two Supreme Court seats that were open. "It is my belief," she wrote, "that the citizens of this nation would warmly accept appointment of a woman to the Supreme Court." She told the president that the Supreme Court of the state of Arizona had a long-serving woman, Lorna Lockwood, on its bench. Lockwood was elected to the court in 1960 and had become its chief justice in 1965. O'Connor continued in her letter, "The citizens of Arizona have demonstrated their high regard and affection for the [female] member of our court in many statewide elections."

Although her letter went unheeded, O'Connor set aside her remorse that a woman had not been nominated, and threw her support

A LINE OF TRAILBLAZERS

Sandra Day O'Connor, as the first woman justice on the Supreme Court, was certainly a trailblazer for other women to follow. But her own career in the law was made possible by a string of women trailblazers before her.

The first American woman to be admitted to law school was Lemma Barkaloo, of Brooklyn, New York, in 1869. Although she did not graduate, in March 1870, she became the first woman to argue a case in court. The first woman to graduate from law school was Ada H. Kepley of Illinois. She graduated in 1870, but was not admitted to the bar in that state because of her gender. Sarah Killgore Wertman, of Michigan, was the first woman both to graduate from law school and to be admitted to the bar. The first woman licensed to practice law in the United States was Iowa's Arabelle A. Mansfield, in 1869. Esther McQuigg Morris served as the country's first female justice of the peace, at the South Pass Mining Camp in Wyoming Territory, in 1870. She is said to have briefly jailed her own husband when he caused a disruption in her courtroom.

Before O'Connor's rise to the Supreme Court, the woman who rose highest in the U.S. judicial system was Florence

Ellinwood Allen (1884–1966). Allen was the first woman in Ohio to become a public prosecutor, the first woman in Ohio to sit on a common pleas court, the first woman on the Ohio Supreme Court, the first woman on the U.S. Court of Appeals, and the first woman to serve as chief judge of a federal court of appeals.

Like O'Connor, Allen was born in the West, in Salt Lake City, Utah. She was the daughter of Clarence E. Allen, Utah's first congressman, and Corrine Tuckerman Allen, the first woman to enroll in Smith College (in Massachusetts). Florence Allen became the first woman judge in the United States to preside over a first-degree murder trial and the first woman judge to impose the death penalty on a convicted murderer. Eleanor Roosevelt, the wife of President Franklin D. Roosevelt, once wrote that if a president of the United States "should decide to nominate a woman for the Supreme Court, it should be Judge Allen." Allen herself was not confident that this would happen in her lifetime, and when she died in 1966, American women were still fifteen years away from seeing one of their own on the highest court in the land.

behind Nixon's choice. The day after hearing about Rehnquist's nomination, O'Connor took to the floor of the Arizona senate chamber and publicly professed her admiration for Rehnquist, describing him as "one of the most brilliant legal minds in the country." She recounted their law school days together, saying that he "appeared to be head and shoulders above everyone else in the class in terms of pure legal ability."[18] Although she joked that she regretted that the nominee "doesn't wear a skirt," she did go on to predict that one day Rehnquist would become the chief justice of the Supreme Court.[19] (Rehnquist was sworn in as an associate justice of the Supreme Court on January 7, 1972. O'Connor witnessed the ceremony. Her prediction came true when President Ronald Reagan elevated Rehnquist to the top job on the nation's highest court on September 26, 1986.)

JUDGE O'CONNOR

O'Connor entered the judiciary when she decided to run for a seat on the Maricopa County Superior Court in 1974. She narrowly won election and served for five years, hearing arguments in civil and criminal cases, instructing juries, and rendering decisions. She loved the job immediately. It gave her life control, organization, and discipline, familiar characteristics of her upbringing.

In 1979 Arizona governor Bruce Babbitt, a Democrat, appointed O'Connor to the twenty-two-member Arizona Court of Appeals. Among its responsibilities, the court considers appeals of civil decisions handed down in the state's superior courts. O'Connor spent eighteen months on the court. Her colleagues considered her written opinions thoughtful and well reasoned. McFeatters reported, "Of her twenty-nine opinions . . . none indicated her opinions on controversial constitutional issues such as abortion, busing as a way to desegregate [public] schools, school prayer, the death penalty, affirmative action, or the rights of criminals." O'Connor, perhaps aspiring to an even higher court, probably knew that publishing her personal opinions on such debatable issues could come back to haunt her in a future confirmation hearing, which might cause her to be rejected as a nominee.

While serving on the state court of appeals, O'Connor supported the founding of the National Association of Women Judges (NAWJ). Among its goals the NAWJ seeks to ensure equal justice and access to the court system for all, "including women, youth, the elderly, minorities, the underprivileged, and people with disabilities" and to increase "the number of women on the bench in order for the judiciary to more accurately reflect the role of women in a democratic society." Just two years after its formation in 1979, the organization represented half the nation's eight hundred female jurists, who made up 5 percent of the nation's judges. O'Connor was named the organization's first "Judge of the Year."

With Sandra on the prestigious court of appeals and John working as a successful lawyer at a private law firm, the O'Connors enjoyed the best that Phoenix high society had to offer. They frequented country club dinners, polo matches, golf tournaments, and charity benefits. They enjoyed discussing politics and the law with friends, who openly speculated about O'Connor's future as the first woman justice of the Supreme Court. (Republican friends had also tried, in 1978, to convince her to run for governor, but she showed little interest in the position.) Sandra had thrived in the powerful and intriguing world of the state senate, but she did not seem to aspire to higher political office. She did, however, have a strong desire to make contributions to society, especially for women. She would have her chance when President Reagan came calling.

CHAPTER FOUR

Reagan's Choice

O N JANUARY 20, 1981, Ronald Wilson Reagan took the oath of office as the fortieth president of the United States. The former Hollywood actor and governor of California spent two terms in office, from 1981 to 1989. The previous fall, prior to the general election in November, Republican candidate Reagan held a press conference to respond to negative attacks launched by the Democrat candidate and current president, Jimmy Carter. Most Americans viewed Carter as a weak and indecisive leader. Frustrated voters considered Carter's presidency largely a failure, mainly because of his inability to solve the country's economic woes and to secure the release of fifty-one American hostages who were being held captive in Iran. Carter's campaign was growing increasingly desperate to find a way to defeat the popular Reagan, who was supported by Republicans and Democrats alike.

To answer the attacks of the Carter campaign, Reagan held a press conference in Los Angeles, California, on October 14, 1980. He said:

A number of false and misleading accusations have been made in this campaign. . . . One of the accusations has been that I am somehow opposed to full and equal opportunities for women in America. . . . I am announcing today that one of the first Supreme Court vacancies in my administration will be filled by the most qualified woman I can find.

President Ronald Reagan and his wife, Nancy, wave to the crowds as they ride down Pennsylvania Avenue toward the White House during the Inaugural Parade held in Washington, D.C., on January 20, 1981.

The announcement made the front page of nearly every newspaper in America. The *New York Times* called it "a bold move." President Carter's campaign dismissed the pledge as an empty promise intended to gain women's votes. First Lady Rosalynn Carter claimed that her husband had planned for quite some time to put a woman on the Court if a vacancy arose during his presidency (but none did). Reagan's vow to put a woman on the Court, as well as his effective performance two weeks later at the only debate between him and Carter, helped him surge ahead in the polls. On Election Day in November, voters swept Reagan into office. By then his promise to put a woman on the Court had been nearly forgotten by the public, but Reagan remembered and meant to keep his word at the first available opportunity. He wouldn't have long to wait.

AN OPENING ON THE COURT

On March 26, 1981, Supreme Court justice Potter Stewart had a private meeting at his Washington, D.C., home with Attorney General William French Smith. (Smith was the former law partner who had interviewed O'Connor back in 1952, and told her she could get a job only as a secretary.) Coincidentally March 26 was O'Connor's fifty-first birthday. The meeting had been arranged by George H. W. Bush, who was then vice president of the United States. Stewart, age sixty-six, had been appointed to the Supreme Court by President Dwight D. Eisenhower in 1958. Stewart told Smith that he had decided to retire in June, when the Court's term was over. Stewart wanted his decision to be made known to President Reagan, so Reagan would have plenty of time to find a successor. However, Stewart wanted his decision kept quiet until June.

The following day Smith asked an assistant named Ken Starr to quietly begin researching a list of potential Supreme Court nominees. Smith said that his office should prepare for a Court vacancy in the summer, but did not mention his conversation with Justice Stewart. Biskupic observed, "It had been six years since the last Supreme Court appointment, and all but two of the justices were over [sixty-five], so Smith's request [would not have seemed unusual to Starr]." Working with a White House lawyer named Fred Fielding, Smith had already written a few names on a piece of paper.

When Smith handed the paper to Starr, Starr asked, "'Who's O'Connor? All you've got here is a last name.'

'That's Sandra Day O'Connor,' Smith said. 'She's an appeals court judge in Arizona.'" Smith did not know much more about her than that. A few other women's names were on the list, along with those of some men.

DELAYED GRATIFICATION

Smith planned to tell President Reagan in a few more days that there would soon be a Supreme Court nomination to make. But on Monday, March 30, the president was shot outside a Washington, D.C., hotel by a would-be assassin. The bullet hit Reagan under his left arm, narrowly missing a vital artery, and lodged in his left lung. He was rushed to the hospital, where he underwent emergency surgery that saved his life.

Reagan was back in the White House two weeks later, "but it was not until April 21, nearly a month after Smith's conversation with Justice Stewart, that the attorney general thought the president was sufficiently recovered to hear of the impending Court vacancy," wrote Biskupic. Smith gave the news to Reagan in the president's private study on the third floor of the White House. Biskupic continued, "The president, remembering his campaign promise, expressed his preference for a female nominee." Smith assured the president that a search was under way and that women were included in the search.

THE FOCUS NARROWS

O'Connor's résumé did not necessarily make her the ideal candidate for the nomination. She was not on a federal court, or even the highest court in a state, from which many previous justices had come. Instead she was a judge on a state intermediate court, handling the appeals in civil and criminal cases. But she was also a former state office holder, with deep and well-maintained connections to the Republican Party. Among her activities, in 1971, she had formed a vast network of support for her law school classmate and good friend William Rehnquist's Supreme Court nomination. In 1972 she cochaired President Richard Nixon's reelection campaign in Arizona. She was friends with Barry Goldwater, whose conservatism had won over millions of Americans. Reagan had brought Goldwater's conservatism to Washington. She was also close friends with Chief Justice Warren Burger, whom she and John had met on a vacation to Utah in 1979. Biskupic acknowledged that Burger had been so impressed by O'Connor that he "had appointed her to judicial commissions that gave her exposure in national and even international legal circles."

O'Connor also stood out at a time when Republican women were a rarity on state and federal courts. When Justice Stewart announced his retirement from the Supreme Court on June 18, 1981, the media immediately focused on the few women judges who were also Republicans. Cornelia Kennedy, a judge on the U.S. Circuit Court of Appeals; Joan Dempsey Klein, a judge on the Los Angeles Superior Court; and, of course, O'Connor, were among them.

A Justice Department lawyer named F. Henry Habicht had the task of researching O'Connor's personal life and legal opinions. All nominees to federal positions must go through this discovery process, in order to ensure that only the most upstanding candidates are considered for a job. Habicht went to Phoenix to look up legislation O'Connor had sponsored as a state senator and to interview her former colleagues in the state legislature, to learn more about O'Connor and her positions on certain political issues. Because news of Stewart's retirement was common knowledge, and because judicial insiders considered O'Connor to be a prospective candidate, it wasn't long before Habicht's presence was reported to O'Connor. Habicht, who had already read through all of O'Connor's judicial writings, was impressed by her accomplishments. Her colleagues in Phoenix spoke in glowing terms of her professional integrity and personal warmth, further convincing Habicht that O'Connor would come across well in Senate confirmation hearings. Years later he would convey his feelings:

 I felt like we had the whole package [in O'Connor].

Next Attorney General Smith asked Ken Starr to visit O'Connor in Phoenix. (Starr also interviewed Judge Cornelia Kennedy in Detroit, Michigan, who was also being considered for the vacant Supreme Court seat.) Biskupic reported, "The White House wanted to keep the selection process a secret to make sure that any flaw in a potential nominee's background could be found first by the administration, rather than the press or a hostile member of the Senate" (whose members vote to confirm Supreme Court nominees). Smith later wrote in his memoir about the importance of the screening process for judicial nominees. He described one candidate for a judgeship who had failed to file her income taxes for a number of years. A person who knowingly breaks the law does not make a good candidate for any federal position. Writing specifically about the search for a candidate to fill the 1981 Supreme Court vacancy, Smith described candidates who looked good on paper, but "on closer inspection, [they had] oversized skeletons in their closets."

On June 23 Smith told Reagan about the leading candidates. Having already been acquainted with O'Connor's work, the president was most interested in knowing more about her. He immediately felt a connection to her western heritage. Although he was born in Illinois, Reagan had adopted a western state, California, as his home and lived on a ranch—riding horses, chopping wood, clearing trails, and building fences. O'Connor quickly became a leading candidate for the job.

Two days later, on June 25, Smith called O'Connor for the first time. She was not surprised, because she had already heard that the administration was investigating her. Smith told O'Connor that she was being considered for a federal position. O'Connor, in the blithe manner that had come to characterize her personality, joked,

" It must be a secretarial position, is it not?

Smith did not respond to O'Connor's obvious allusion to her job interview with him nearly thirty years earlier. Ken Starr and another aide interviewed O'Connor in person two days later. Starr had no idea at the time that O'Connor was recovering from major surgery. It was typical of O'Connor not to allow a personal concern—or physical discomfort—to distract her from her professional duty. On June 29 O'Connor traveled to Washington, D.C., for meetings with a variety of administration officials who would be vital to her candidacy, including President Reagan.

MEETING THE PRESIDENT

O'Connor met Reagan in the Oval Office just after ten o'clock in the morning on July 1, 1981. Attorney General Smith and other members of the administration were present as well. O'Connor and Reagan talked about horses and ranch life. The two discovered that they had more in common than life in the West. Biskupic recounted, "Both had had somewhat isolated childhoods. They each had developed rarely revealed inner lives and, in their early public careers, had been underestimated."[14] They also discovered that they were both practical, optimistic, and their careers had benefited from their tenacity, hard work, and good timing. Forty-five minutes after they were introduced to one another, Reagan was convinced that he had found his nominee. O'Connor was not so sure.

Years later O'Connor recalled boarding a plane back home to Arizona after her meeting with Reagan. She did not think she would be chosen as the nominee. After all an Arizonan, William Rehnquist, was already seated on the Court. The Court doesn't usually have two or more members who come from the same state. O'Connor did not believe that she would be chosen, and said she felt relieved.

Five days after they met in person, Reagan telephoned O'Connor to tell her of his intention to announce her nomination to the Supreme Court. O'Connor said later that she was "thunderstruck . . . and very

President Reagan introduces his Supreme Court nominee, Sandra Day O'Connor, to members of the press on July 15, 1981, in the White House's Rose Garden.

concerned, because it's a very hard job." The nomination was not only O'Connor's chance to sit on the high court. It was also an opportunity for her to break nearly two hundred years of the tradition of male members on the Court. The following day Reagan made it official: at a press conference announcing O'Connor's nomination, the president said she possessed "the unique qualities of temperament, fairness, intellectual capacity, and devotion to the public good" that had been characteristics of all those who had preceded her on the Court.

MEDIA FRENZY AND CONFIRMATION

O'Connor was not prepared for the media frenzy that followed. She was swarmed by reporters, and TV cameras transmitted her every public move. Her name was suddenly being mentioned in households across the country and pictures of her and her family appeared in countless newspapers and magazines. The excitement came largely from the novelty of O'Connor's being a woman.

However, not everyone was pleased with the choice. Some who believed a woman's place was in the home opposed the nomination. Others focused their criticism not on O'Connor's gender, but on her qualifications. Critics argued that she was unqualified because she had been an appeals court judge for only eighteen months. They considered her to be neither an exceptional lawyer nor a legal scholar, and her judicial opinions were not particularly notable. Further the hot-button topics of the time were abortion and equal rights, and many expressed concern about O'Connor's positions on those issues. They wondered how she would rule on related cases heard by the Court. Hers could be a decisive vote, potentially bringing monumental changes to American society. Regardless of the criticism, a nationwide poll conducted in mid-July 1981 found that 86 percent of those questioned approved of a woman serving on the Court. Sixty-nine percent believed O'Connor to be qualified to serve on the Court.

O'Connor's Senate confirmation hearings began on September 18, 1981. Supreme Court nominations—and confirmations—are largely based in politics. Republican or conservative presidents tend to choose nominees who reflect their values. The same is true of Democrat or liberal presidents. As a result of the politics involved, Republicans on the Senate Judiciary Committee tended to support O'Connor. Democrats tended not to. There was so much public interest in O'Connor's nomination that her hearing marked the first time a Senate confirmation hearing was televised. Over the course of three days, O'Connor answered senators' questions about her positions on the Constitution, abortion, equal rights,

CONFIRMING A JUSTICE

Article II of the U.S. Constitution gives the president the power to appoint judges of the Supreme Court, with the "Advice and Consent of the Senate." The Constitution does not place qualifications for serving as a justice, so the president may nominate anyone for the Court. However, that person must receive Senate confirmation.

Judicial nominees first appear before the Senate Judiciary Committee, formally called the United States Senate Committee on the Judiciary. The committee, one of the oldest in the Senate, was created in 1816 and is comprised of nineteen members. The majority party in the Senate has the most members on the committee. For example, in 2011, the Democrat Party had more members in the Senate than any other political party. As a result ten of the committee's eighteen members were Democrats. The committee conducts hearings on whether to confirm prospective federal judges, including Supreme Court justices. Hearings can be contentious, often as a result of political game-playing during which the party that opposes the president debates a candidate's qualifications and fitness for service on a federal court.

During the hearings senators ask nominees tough questions on a variety of contemporary subjects, including how the nominee interprets the Constitution and what the nominee believes about issues such as abortion rights, gun rights, equal rights, and more. After the hearings have been completed, a simple majority vote is required to confirm or reject a nominee. If the committee confirms a nominee, the vote then moves to the full Senate. Rejections are quite rare. In its history the Senate has rejected only twelve Supreme Court nominees. Once the Senate confirms a nominee, the president must sign a document called a commission. The commission must have the seal of the Department of Justice affixed to it before the new justice can be sworn in.

When the Senate is in recess, the president may appoint a judge to a federal court, including the Supreme Court, without the advice and consent of the Senate. However, the appointment can last only until the end of the next Senate session (which usually means no more than two years). In order to continue to serve, the appointee must be confirmed by the Senate.

Sandra Day O'Connor waves from the steps of the Capitol after her unanimous
confirmation to the Supreme Court by the U.S. Senate on September 21, 1981.

busing to achieve desegregation in public schools, the death penalty, and other issues. Like all Supreme Court nominees, O'Connor was careful not to reveal too much in her answers. She insisted that her personal feelings on any given case would not influence her judicial opinions. At times O'Connor felt impatient because of the senators' endless questioning. She kept her impatience to herself, however, and on September 21, the full U.S. Senate confirmed her nomination by a vote of 99 to 0. (Montana senator Max Baucus was not present when the vote was taken.)

Shortly after her confirmation, an elated O'Connor stood on the steps of the U.S. Capitol with Vice President George H. W. Bush and several senators who had supported her nomination. Biskupic related O'Connor's comments to reporters and visitors who were looking up at her: "'I am absolutely overjoyed at the expression of support from the Senate.'" The full meaning of the moment—and of O'Connor's place in history as the first woman justice on the Supreme Court—was not lost to anyone who witnessed that moment, least of all O'Connor herself.

CHAPTER FIVE

Supreme Swing Vote

W ITH THE NEWLY SWORN-IN O'CONNOR as the newest member of the Supreme Court— the justices are sometimes casually referred to as "the Supremes"—it was time to focus on the business at hand. O'Connor, who had always been skilled at shutting out distractions, tried to ignore her celebrity status and settle in to her new life. (In her first year on the Court, she received 60,000 letters from the public, more than any other justice in history.) In the preface to her 2003 book, *The Majesty of the Law: Reflections of a Supreme Court Justice*, she wrote that when she began her service on the Court:

> (John and I) looked forward to the many new experiences— both personal and professional—we were sure to have: enjoying new and wonderful friends; meeting with Presidents, Vice Presidents, cabinet members, ambassadors, and other Justices and judges from around the world; travel to each of the fifty states and sometimes to other countries for speeches and meetings; and most important, I looked forward to the privilege of applying myself to work worth doing, addressing the toughest legal issues in our nation.

Sandra Day O'Connor on the steps of the U.S. Supreme Court in September 1981. Pictured (*from left*) are: O'Connor's father, Harry Day; John O'Connor; O'Connor's mother, Ada Mae; O'Connor; Chief Justice Warren Burger; and O'Connor's sons, Brian, Jay, and Scott.

O'Connor's first day of work as a Supreme Court justice was September 28, 1981. At a meeting of the justices that morning, she was given a list of one thousand petitions for Court review. She would need to participate in deciding which cases the Court would agree to hear. Although some Court-watchers wondered if she would be intimidated by her prestigious new surroundings and colleagues, she took little time to prove that she was not. In her first oral argument a few days later, a case involving California's attempt to obtain an offshore oil and natural gas leasing system, she asked her first official question as a justice.

In addition to oral arguments—hourly sessions held every Monday, Tuesday, and Wednesday during the Court's term—in which lawyers for each side argue the merits of their case, the justices' work also included screening those requests for review, studying papers of cases that had been accepted for review, and crafting decisions for cases that had already been heard.

Ideally justices should be independent and nonpartisan, and should make up their minds based on the individual merits of each case they hear. In practical terms, however, the justices do tend to base their decisions on conservative or liberal ideological viewpoints that they already possess. When O'Connor joined the Court, decisions generally were split between conservatives and liberals. Four justices were considered conservative: Chief Justice Warren Burger, William Rehnquist, Byron White, and Lewis Powell. Four justices were considered liberal: William Brennan, Harry Blackmun, Thurgood Marshall, and John Paul Stevens. O'Connor became the tiebreaker, and her vote was called a swing vote. That is, although she proved to be conservative on many economic and governmental issues, she was liberal on many social issues. So neither liberals nor conservatives on the Court could count on her vote. As a result hers was often the deciding vote on many landmark cases. (Her swing vote status would continue as, over the years, new justices joined the Court to replace former ones: conservatives Anthony Kennedy, Clarence Thomas, and Antonin Scalia; and liberals David Souter, Ruth Bader Ginsburg, and Stephen Breyer.)

NOTEWORTHY CASES

In her career as a Supreme Court justice, Sandra Day O'Connor heard arguments for well over one hundred cases. As she developed a reputation as a swing vote, Court-watchers and the legal community were

This official photograph of the members of the U.S. Supreme Court was taken in 1990. Seated (*left to right*) are: Justice Harry Blackmun; Justice Byron White; Chief Justice William Rehnquist; Justice Thurgood Marshall; Justice John Paul Stevens. Standing (*left to right*) are: Justice Anthony Kennedy; Justice O'Connor; Justice Antonin Scalia; and Justice David Souter.

THE MARBLE PALACE

The Supreme Court building, which was built between 1932 and 1935, is located in Washington, D.C., across from the U.S. Capitol. It was designed by prominent American architect Cass Gilbert, who died a year before its completion.

Rising four stories aboveground, the exterior of the building and much of its interior are made of marble quarried from Vermont, Alabama, and Georgia. The courtroom itself is lined with Spanish marble and the twenty-four columns inside the courtroom are made from Italian marble. At the west entrance of the building (the side facing the Capitol), sixteen marble columns support the portico. At the top of the columns is an area called the architrave, which is inscribed with the Supreme Court's motto, "Equal Justice Under Law." Above the architrave a triangular space called the pediment is filled with a sculpture by Robert Aiken. The sculpture is called *Liberty Enthroned Guarded by Order and Authority*. The bronze doors of the west and east entrances were sculpted by John Donnelly Jr., and depict historic scenes in the development of the law.

Like the west entrance, the east entrance is lined with sixteen marble columns. The architrave bears the words "Justice the Guardian of Liberty." The pediment contains a sculpture by Herman McNeil that represents great lawgivers in history—Moses, Confucius, and Solon. According to a description provided by the National Parks Service, "The lawgivers are surrounded by groups that represent Means of Enforcing the Law, Tempering Justice with Mercy, Carrying on Civilization, and Settlement of Disputes Between States."

On the north side of the building is a seated figure called *The Contemplation of Justice*. The seated figure on the south side is called *The Authority of Law*. Inside the courtroom marble sculptures called friezes make up the south and north walls. The south wall frieze includes figures of ancient lawgivers, including Moses, Solomon, Confucius, and Augustus. The frieze on the north wall depicts lawgivers from the Middle Ages onward, and includes Justinian, Charlemagne, William Blackstone, and Napoleon.

The basement of the building contains the parking garage and mailroom. The ground floor, or first floor, is made up of a public information office, exhibit halls that are open to visitors, a cafeteria, a gift shop, and an administrative office. On the second floor are the Great Hall, which contains marble busts of the Court's chief justices; the courtroom; and the justices' chambers. On the third floor are offices of the justices' law clerks, the legal office, and the justices' dining room and reading room. The Court library is located on the fourth floor. The Supreme Court gym, which includes a basketball court, is located on the fifth floor.

The west side of the U.S. Supreme Court building

often kept guessing how she would vote in any given case.

In a 2001 *New York Times Magazine* article, law professor and columnist Jeffrey Rosen wrote, "O'Connor forces the Court and those who follow it to engage in a guessing game about her wishes in case after case." However, as the swing vote on the Court, "O'Connor is in the majority more often than any of her colleagues," asserted Ramesh Ponnuru, in a 2003 article for *National Review.* Indeed O'Connor's unpredictability eventually put her in a powerful position on the Court. Ponnuru continued, "given the power the Supreme Court has assumed, O'Connor has become the most powerful woman in America. Excluding foreign policy, indeed, one could even say that she is the most powerful person in America."Although the following list is not comprehensive, some of her more noteworthy cases follow.

Webster v. Reproductive Health Services

Since long before the Supreme Court asserted in Roe v. Wade (1973) that the U.S. Constitution includes a right to privacy which extends to a woman's desire to have an abortion, with some restrictions, abortion has been a hot-button topic in the United States. There has been little middle ground between those who support the Court's decision in that case and those who do not.

A 1989 case that came before the Court, called *Webster v. Reproductive Health Services*, drew a great deal of attention from the American public and the media because the Court's decision in this case had the potential to overturn *Roe v. Wade*. In 1986 the state of Missouri enacted legislation that placed a number of restrictions on abortion. The law stated that "[t]he life of each human being begins at conception," and imposed the following restrictions: State employees and state facilities could not be used in performing or assisting abortions that were not necessary to save the mother's life; encouragement and counseling to have abortions was prohibited; and, beginning in the twentieth week of pregnancy, doctors were required to perform tests to determine whether a fetus could survive outside the womb. Lower courts had struck down the law, and it was brought before the Supreme Court in 1989. In a 5-4 decision, the Court ultimately ruled to uphold the state law. O'Connor played an important role in the decision, voting with the majority to allow Missouri's restrictions on the abortion procedure.

United States v. Lopez

On March 10, 1992, Alfonso Lopez Jr., a high school senior in San Antonio, Texas, brought a concealed .38-caliber revolver and five cartridges into his public school. School officials confronted him and Lopez admitted to having the gun. He was charged with violating the federal Gun-Free School Zones Act of 1990, which prohibited the possession and discharge of firearms near public schools.

Attorneys for Lopez filed suit to dismiss the charges against him on the grounds that the Gun-Free School Zones Act was unconstitutional because the Constitution does not allow Congress to pass laws controlling public schools. Meanwhile Lopez was tried and convicted of the crime and appealed his conviction in federal court. The federal court overturned Lopez's conviction, agreeing that the Gun-Free School Zones Act was unconstitutional. The case worked its way up to the Supreme Court, where it was argued in late 1994. Five months later the Court announced its decision. In another close vote (5-4), the Supreme Court agreed that the law was unconstitutional. O'Connor's was the deciding vote.

Boy Scouts of America v. Dale

In 2000 a case called *Boy Scouts of America v. Dale* reached the Court.

The Boy Scouts of America is a private, nonprofit organization that instills its system of values in boys. "It asserts that homosexuality is inconsistent with those values," reported Linda Greenhouse, a writer for the *New York Times*. James Dale was a Scoutmaster in New Jersey until the organization learned that he was openly gay and an active gay rights advocate. Dale was expelled from the Boy Scouts, so he sued the organization for discrimination based on sexual orientation, which is prohibited in New Jersey. The New Jersey Supreme Court ruled that the Boy Scouts had violated state law by rescinding Dale's membership.

The Boy Scouts appealed the state court's ruling to the next highest authority—the U.S. Supreme Court. In another tight decision— once again O'Connor's deciding vote made the ruling 5-4—the Court reversed the previous decision, ruling in favor of the Boy Scouts. The Court ruled that the lower court had violated the Boy Scouts' constitutional right to freedom of association, which allows a private organization to exclude a person from membership when "the presence of that person affects in a significant way the group's ability to advocate public or private viewpoints." The Court ruled that opposition to homosexuality is part of the Boy Scouts of America's teachings and allowing homosexuals as adult leaders would interfere with those teachings. Therefore the Boy Scouts could not legally be forced to include homosexuals as Scoutmasters.

Bush v. Gore

In one of the most highly anticipated Court decisions in U.S. history, O'Connor cast the deciding vote in one of the rulings handed down in the hotly contested case of *Bush v. Gore*. In the 2000 presidential election, Texas governor George W. Bush was the Republican candidate, running against Vice President Al Gore Jr., the Democrats' candidate. In the United States presidential elections are decided by the Electoral College. Each state has a committee of electors who together make up the college. The number of electors is based on the number of people who represent the state in Congress. Voters cast their ballots for a candidate, and the members of the Electoral College award the state's electoral votes to the candidate who garnered the most votes in that state. A presidential candidate needs 270 electoral votes to win the presidency. By the time Election Day—November 7, 2000—was over, the race was too close to call. It all came down to Florida's electoral votes. The candidate who won those votes would win the presidency.

After a mandatory statewide recount that was required because the race was so close, Bush won by a mere 327 votes. Weeks of recounts in some Florida counties and legal wrangling followed. Meanwhile the results of the mandatory statewide recount were made official by Florida's secretary of state on November 14. With Florida's electoral votes awarded to Bush, he had a total of 271 electoral votes, making him the next president. However, recounts continued in a few Florida counties. Volunteers examined ballots in an attempt to determine voters' intent.

On December 8, the Florida Supreme Court ordered another statewide recount. After lawyers for Bush appealed to the U.S. Supreme Court, the following day the Court ordered the recount stopped until the justices could hear arguments from both sides. On December 11 lawyers for Bush and Gore argued their positions in the Court.

On December 12, the Court ruled 7-2 (O'Connor was in the majority) that it was illegal for the Florida Supreme Court to create a new election law by demanding another recount. (The Florida Supreme Court is the judicial branch of the state's government. The judicial branch cannot make laws. The legislative branch makes laws. Therefore only the legislature could call for another statewide recount, which it did not.) In a separate, 5–4 ruling (again, O'Connor was in the majority), the Court found the lack of uniform, statewide rules for conducting recounts to be troubling. With each county conducting the recount according to its own rules, there was a wide disparity in how recount volunteers interpreted ballots. As a result volunteers who tended to favor Bush would "find" votes for him. Likewise volunteers who were rooting for a Gore victory would "discover" votes for him. The Court ruled that without a single set of standards, it was probable that some Florida voters would be disenfranchised, or denied the right to have their vote counted. Disenfranchisement violates the U.S. Constitution. The Court's rulings meant that the secretary of state's certified results would stand, and George W. Bush took the presidential oath of office in January 2001.

Grutter v. Bollinger

When the University of Michigan Law School denied admission to a highly qualified student named Barbara Grutter, she filed suit against the university, claiming that the university's affirmative action admissions policy resulted in discrimination. Affirmative action policies take into account race, gender, ethnicity, religion, and national origin in order to benefit underrepresented groups, such as women, blacks, and Hispanics, to increase the inclusion of these groups in employment, education, and business. The university admitted that it relies on affirmative action to achieve diversity in its student body. Grutter's complaint claimed that the university's affirmative action policy resulted in "reverse discrimination" because she was white.

In a 5–4 decision in which O'Connor's is the deciding vote, the Court ruled in favor of the university (Bollinger). The Court found that the university's law school considered more important factors—such as grade point average and test scores—in its review of applicants. In other words race was not the only factor upon which the university accepted students. Therefore the Court found that the university did not discriminate against Grutter. (Interestingly, in a separate case heard concurrently with *Grutter*, called *Gratz v. Bollinger*, and decided on the same day as *Grutter*, the Court ruled 6–3 that the University of Michigan's point system for undergraduate admissions, which awarded extra points on the basis of an applicant's minority status, was arbitrary and therefore discriminatory against whites. O'Connor voted with the majority in that case, as well.)

Barbara Grutter (*left*) and Jennifer Gratz (*center*) talk to reporters outside the Supreme Court on April 1, 2003, following the announcement of the Court's decisions in their cases.

During the course of O'Connor's tenure as a Supreme Court justice, she ruled on important and controversial issues such as abortion, affirmative action, and the death penalty, thereby indirectly affecting the lives of millions of everyday Americans. She had been an inspiration to millions of women and girls, both at home and abroad. She was the subject of countless biographical books and articles, and was often included on lists of the most-admired women in America.

Beginning in the 1990s rumors sometimes circulated that she would soon retire, but O'Connor always dismissed them. So it came as a surprise when, on June 30, 2005, she sent a letter to President Bush announcing her retirement after more than twenty-four years on the Court. The three-sentence letter was typical of her direct, no-nonsense style. In the letter she told Bush that she felt privileged to have served on the Court and she would "leave it with enormous respect for [its integrity] and its role in our constitutional structure." When the president announced O'Connor's retirement, he said in his remarks that she had exceeded the expectations that most Americans had of her when she was first named to the Court, and had excelled in the performance of her duties as a justice.

> **This great lady, the president said, . . . became one of the most admired Americans of our time. She leaves an outstanding record of service to the United States, and our nation is deeply grateful.**

O'Connor's fellow justice, Antonin Scalia, observed, "'I don't think [the justice chosen to replace O'Connor will be] any more pleasant or amiable and intent on keeping a good attitude at the Court [than O'Connor was].'"Although over the years, in challenging cases, O'Connor was sometimes at ideological odds with her Supreme Court colleagues, she left with their respect for all she had achieved in her distinguished career.

CHAPTER SIX

Raising the Bar

A FTER SERVING AS A JUSTICE FOR twenty-four years, four months, and six days, O'Connor's retirement from the Supreme Court became official in 2006. Any member of the Court lives his or her life in the public eye. As the first woman on the Court, O'Connor's life was, at times, more closely followed than that of any other justice in history. It was a trade-off she knew she was making when she accepted President Reagan's nomination back in 1981, but there were countless times over the years when she wished she were not so well known. During her tenure on the Court, she endured many life-changing events that tested her vast abilities to cope, including the death of her father, Harry, in 1984; being diagnosed with breast cancer in 1988; and her mother Ada Mae's death in 1989.

In 1993 she welcomed the second woman on the Supreme Court (Ruth Bader Ginsburg), and hoped that the presence of another woman on the Court would diminish the glare of the media spotlight. It did, but only temporarily. In 1994 O'Connor's brother Alan sold the last remaining piece of the Lazy B, the ranch that had been in the O'Connor family for well over a hundred years. It was difficult for O'Connor to imagine never again setting foot on the soil of her beloved childhood home. At the time she said of the sale, "I feel like part of my heart and soul is gone." As always, though, O'Connor met each challenge with the knowledge that life is constantly changing, and she made the best of every circumstance.

International travel was among the activities Sandra and John O'Connor enjoyed together. Here, they pause atop the Great Wall of China, in 1987.

THE BIG C

In 1988 O'Connor was diagnosed with breast cancer. However, she did not speak publicly about it for another six years. Part of O'Connor's treatment included a mastectomy, surgical removal of her cancerous breast. The day before the surgery, O'Connor was scheduled to deliver a speech at a university 200 miles (322 km) from her home near Washington, D.C. She made the six-hour round-trip by car, gave the speech, had the surgery the next day, and was back at work ten days later. She had chemotherapy treatments on Friday mornings, rested during the weekend, and returned to work on Mondays, never missing a single day of work. She did not tell her brother and sister about her cancer until after the surgery. When she did, she was her usual stoic and confident self, expressing certainty that she would survive the disease.

In 1994 O'Connor began speaking publicly about her cancer ordeal. In a speech to the National Coalition for Cancer Survivorship, she described the process by which she, like any other breast cancer patient, began her journey through cancer: with medical exams, X-rays, mammograms, CT scans, and biopsies. She went on to say:

> I was told I had a potentially fatal disease. Now that gets your attention. The Big C. The word cancer [is overwhelming]. I couldn't believe it. I was unprepared for the enormous emotional jolt I received from the diagnosis. All of a sudden my face, my hands, my whole body tingled. It couldn't be true. I was too busy. I feel fine. You can't be serious.

O'Connor went on to speak candidly of her concern about losing her hair, a side effect of chemotherapy. She told her audience that she asked her hairdresser to help her find a wig that most closely matched her natural hairstyle and color, by then blondish-gray. O'Connor was most worried about the reaction of the media and the public, whether they would speculate over her chances of survival, and what they would say about her appearance while she was undergoing treatment. Knowing that so much attention would be focused on her was stressful for a woman who strives to keep her private life private. Biskupic wrote, "But with her usual burst of optimism after a setback, she said to her fellow survivors, 'Is there an upside to all of this? Yes. It made me value each and every day of life more than ever before.'" In another speech about her cancer, she said the experience taught her to "appreciate and treasure each day because you don't know how many more you'll be given, so make those that you have count." She also said she was grateful to have work to distract her from her own troubles.

LIFE AFTER THE COURT

As perhaps the best-known member of the Court, O'Connor had traveled the country and the world to discuss the law and what it's like to serve on the nation's highest court. Over the years she had been a kind of ambassador, not only for the Court, but for how the American judicial system works. Whenever she accepted an invitation to a meeting or conference, her appearance was almost guaranteed to draw a large audience.

When she retired at age seventy-five, McFeatters wrote, O'Connor was "still full of energy and intellectual curiosity and her legendary passion for her work. . . ." She continued making rounds on the lecture circuit, but she concentrated most of her efforts on reclaiming her private life. Her sons, Scott, Brian, and Jay, were all married, and two of them were living in Arizona. She had six grandchildren and wanted to be more directly involved in her children and grandchildren's lives. Returning to Arizona gave her more time to enjoy her family and to cook (she was always considered a talented gourmet chef). She was also able to continue pursuing her favorite outdoor activities—among them skiing, hiking, fishing, tennis, and golf (she hit her first hole-in-one at the Paradise Valley Country Club in Phoenix on December 17, 2000). Perhaps most important, O'Connor left the Court to care for John, her devoted husband of fifty-three years, who had been diagnosed with Alzheimer's disease some fifteen years before.

A LONG GOOD-BYE TO JOHN

Alzheimer's disease is the most common form of dementia, the progressive loss of memory and physical and mental abilities. Alzheimer's is a fatal brain disease that destroys brain cells, which causes memory loss and confusion. Over time problems with thinking and behavior become severe enough to interfere with work, hobbies, and social interactions. There is no known cure for Alzheimer's disease, which is always fatal. O'Connor's mother and President Reagan both died from complications related to Alzheimer's.

For a time before O'Connor's retirement, only family and close friends knew that John, then seventy years old, had been diagnosed with the disease. O'Connor, while she was still a Supreme Court justice, brought John with her to her chambers, and he accompanied her when she traveled, so she could keep an eye on him. According to Biskupic, as the disease progressed, "John sometimes would forget what to do with a tennis racquet, a golf club, even a fork at

CHICO AND SUSIE

Having already written or collaborated on several books, including *Lazy B*, the 2002 memoir she wrote with her brother Alan about growing up on the ranch, O'Connor knew that freedom from reading endless piles of legal briefs would give her time to write more books, for both adults and children. Her first children's book, *Chico*, got its name from her favorite horse on the Lazy B and was published in 2005. Based on an actual event that occurred when O'Connor was six years old, the book tells the story of the day O'Connor and Chico encountered a rattlesnake on the ranch. O'Connor followed up *Chico* with *Finding Susie* (2009), another autobiographical tale. The main character of this book is a lonely girl named Sandra who lives on a ranch and yearns for a pet to keep her company.

dinner." O'Connor did not reveal publicly how she and others who knew John felt about seeing him confused or disengaged from the goings-on around him. People who had known O'Connor for a long time recognized the sadness of the situation, but marveled about her ability to behave as if nothing was wrong. It must have been heartbreaking for O'Connor to watch helplessly as her husband mentally slipped away from her, but, as always, "she did what she had to do: kept track of John and fulfilled her official duties without missing a beat," noted Biskupic. After her retirement O'Connor continued to care for John until it became necessary to move him into a long-term care medical facility, where he died on November 11, 2009.

Throughout O'Connor's career, awards and honors came pouring in. A comprehensive list of them would fill most of the pages of this book. Some of the most notable, however, include the 1985 Elizabeth Blackwell Award. Named for the first woman doctor in the United States, the award is presented by Hobart and William Smith colleges in New York to a woman who has "demonstrated outstanding service to humankind." In 2000 O'Connor became an honorary graduate of The Citadel, the South Carolina military college that did not graduate its first female cadet until 1999. In 2001 O'Connor became the first recipient of the Carol Los Mansmann Award for outstanding public service. Los Mansmann, a distinguished federal judge and friend of O'Connor's, died of breast cancer in 2002. The State Bar Association of Arizona awarded its Lifetime Achievement Award to O'Connor in 2004. She was inducted into the Texas Women's Hall of Fame in 2008. In 2009 she was among those awarded the Presidential Medal of Freedom, the highest civilian honor in the United States. She was even inducted into the National Cowgirl Hall of Fame in Fort Worth, Texas, in 2002.

Also in 2002 Arizona celebrated its ninetieth year of statehood. As part of the celebration, the state released a list of the ten most important people in state history. The list was made up of politicians, missionaries, scientists, and environmentalists. Sandra Day O'Connor, the only woman on the list, was ranked number eight.

A 9-foot-tall (2.7-meters-tall) bronze statue of O'Connor was erected inside the Sandra Day O'Connor U.S. Courthouse in Phoenix, Arizona, in 2002. While sculptor Susan Henningsen was working on the statue, O'Connor personally invited her to the nation's capital. Henningsen visited O'Connor in her Chevy Chase, Maryland, home, where O'Connor cooked dinner for the artist. Over the course of the next few days, O'Connor posed for photos that Henningsen would later use to make the statue a more accurate depiction of O'Connor. Henningsen later commented that O'Connor was "very sweet to be around." The statue, which weighs 1,000 pounds (454 kilograms), is perched atop a granite pedestal in the courthouse. The hem of O'Connor's judicial robe bears the names of her family members. She is carrying a copy of *U.S. Reports*, the official record of the proceedings of the Supreme Court.

Other buildings named in O'Connor's honor are the Sandra Day O'Connor College of Law at Arizona State University and two schools: the Sandra Day O'Connor High Schools are located in Phoenix, Arizona, and Helotes, Texas. An award, called the Sandra Day O'Connor Award, was established by the Philadelphia Bar Association in 1993. The honor is given annually to a "female attorney who [has] demonstrated superior legal talent, achieved significant legal accomplishments, and furthered the advancement of women in both the profession and the community."

DRAWING AN AUDIENCE

O'Connor turned eighty years old in 2010. At an age when other retirees might be slowing down, O'Connor has lost none of the energy and focus that have been the distinguishing characteristics of her remarkable life. She continues to be a highly sought-after public speaker. She is often asked to deliver commencement speeches, speeches at the dedications of law buildings, and remarks for the honorees of prestigious awards. She maintains her schedule of traveling abroad to speak at international legal conferences.

For O'Connor, two of her most meaningful public appearances came in the early 2000s. Ronald Reagan, the man who was responsible for placing her on the Court, died in 2004. Nearly four thousand of the most politically powerful people in the United States and the world attended his funeral. It was especially moving for O'Connor to know that before Reagan died, he had personally requested that she be among the fewer than ten people who would deliver remarks at his funeral service.

Less than a year later, when O'Connor's dear friend and Supreme Court colleague William Rehnquist succumbed to thyroid cancer, the usually stoic O'Connor could not conceal her emotions. When Rehnquist's casket was carried up the steps of the Supreme Court building, photographers captured images of O'Connor wiping away tears. But the following day O'Connor spoke at Rehnquist's funeral in her usual clear, strong voice, remembering with poignancy and humor their many decades of friendship.

TEACHING OTHERS

One of O'Connor's missions as a jurist was educating others, not only about the law, but about the importance of creating better-skilled and more ethical lawyers. In many of her speeches, dating as far back as 1982, she advocated for increased moral and social responsibility. In one speech she said, "law schools must not only teach students to be competent lawyers but also to [give them a] sense of professional responsibility."

O'Connor has extended her mission to educating young people about how the government works. When a 2008 national study revealed that barely one-third of Americans can name the three branches of government or explain what they do, she was appalled. She is concerned that most U.S. schools no longer teach civics, the study of the U.S. government and the rights and responsibilities of American citizens. To address the need for civics education,

O'Connor founded iCivics Inc., a nonprofit civics education program, in early 2009. Its companion website, OurCourts.org (now called ICivics.org), uses interactive games to teach civics lessons and critical thinking.

"A GOOD JUDGE"

Perhaps more so than anyone else, O'Connor herself is awed by the remarkable life she has lived. She is also immensely proud of all that she has achieved in her lifetime of hard work and discipline. She enjoyed a long, happy marriage to John; she raised three sons who grew up to become successful in their own right; she has grandchildren to spoil; she forged a preeminent career. She says she is happiest at home, where she feels peaceful and content, but is also glad to have activities that keep her busy, and good friends with whom she can share her life. Those who know her best, however, insist that despite her fame and fortune, she has remained remarkably down-to-earth.

When O'Connor was undergoing her Senate confirmation hearings in 1981, she was asked what her epitaph should read.

 Ah, she said. The tombstone question. I hope it says, 'Here lies a good judge.'

Her skill as a judge is rarely debated. O'Connor's brother Alan may have described her best, however, when he said in an interview: "'The essence of Sandra is that if you're around her, the bar is raised in your life. You just feel like doing better things and being a better person.'"

TIMELINE

1930 — Born on March 26 in El Paso, Texas

1936 — Sent to El Paso to attend the Radford School for Girls

1946 — Graduates from Austin High School

1950 — Graduates from Stanford University

1952 — Graduates from Stanford University Law School; marries John O'Connor

1953 — Works for free for the San Mateo County district attorney because she is unable to find full-time work; John joins the army and the couple moves to Germany

1957 — The O'Connors return to Arizona; both are admitted to the state bar; son Scott is born

1958 — Sets up a private law practice with Tom Tobin

1960 — Son Brian is born; O'Connor decides to stay home and raise her children

1962 — Son Jay is born